It's me...
a Rabbit

An imprint of Om Books International

First Published in 2019 by

Om KIDZ | Om Books International

Corporate & Editorial Office
A-12, Sector 64, Noida 201 301
Uttar Pradesh, India
Phone: +91 120 477 4100
Email: editorial@ombooks.com
Website: www.ombooksinternational.com

Sales Office
107, Ansari Road, Darya Ganj
New Delhi 110 002, India
Phone: +91 11 4000 9000
Email: sales@ombooks.com
Website: www.ombooks.com

© Om Books International 2019

ISBN: 978-93-86410-51-1

Printed in India

10 9 8 7 6 5 4 3 2 1

Contents

WHO ARE YOU?

Hello! I am a rabbit. I belong to the Leporidae family of animals. I am a ground dweller and can be found in all types of environments, such as tropical forests, wetlands and deserts.

Scientific Name

Oryctolagus cuniculus

WHAT ARE YOUR UNIQUE FEATURES?

Long Ears

We have long ears, powerful and long hind legs and a short tail. Our long ears help us detect predators. Our tails look like fluffy puffs of fur.

Fluffy Tail

predator - animal that naturally preys on others

A new word to learn

HOW BIG ARE YOU?

Pygmy Rabbit

Small rabbits, such as Pygmy rabbits, can be as tiny as 7.9 inches in length and may weigh less than 0.5 kg. The larger species can grow almost as big as 19.7 inches and might weigh more than 2 kg.

Flemish Giant

WHERE DO YOU LIVE?

Most of us live in burrows. The European rabbit makes the most extensive burrows which are called **warrens**.

Forms

The non-burrowing rabbits make surface nests which are known as forms.

A new word to learn

Warren - network of interconnected rabbit burrows

WHAT DO YOU LIKE TO EAT?

We are herbivores and like to munch on grass, hay, leafy shrubs, fruits, cruciferous plants, clover and herbs. Wild rabbits also eat seeds, twigs and bark.

Our Nutritious Diet

In order to ensure proper nutrition, we must eat plants in large quantities.

DO YOU HAVE A PANORAMIC VISION?

Yes, we can see in all directions. We have excellent vision and a great sense of smell and hearing.

Buck and Doe

A female rabbit is called a doe, while a male rabbit is known as a buck.

ARE YOU A SOCIAL ANIMAL?

European rabbits are the most social rabbits of the lot and they live in groups. They have flexible social behaviour which depends on their **habitat**.

A new word to learn

Habitat - the environment in which an organism lives and where it can find food and shelter

DO YOU HIBERNATE?

A new word
to learn

Nocturnal -
active at night

A new word
to learn

Hibernate - spend
winter in a
dormant state

None of the species of rabbits are known to **hibernate**; they are active throughout the year. They are mostly **nocturnal** creatures.

DO YOU MAKE SOUNDS?

We are relatively silent, except for the loud screams we emit when we are scared. The only exception to this is the Volcano rabbit, which is known to sound off a variety of calls.

Who are Volcano Rabbits?

Volcano rabbits are found in pine forests located in the high mountains around Mexico City.

We use scent, more than sounds, for communication. We have well-developed glands all over our body and we rub them on fixed objects in the environment to show our group identity, age, and territory ownership.

WHAT ARE BABY RABBITS CALLED?

Our babies are called kittens. Our newborns are blind and helpless at birth.

Kittens Grow Rapidly

Kittens grow up very quickly. Male rabbits do not help in raising the babies.

Mother rabbits only nurse their kittens once a day and that too only for a few minutes. However, the mother rabbit's milk makes up for this lack of attention, since the milk is highly nutritious.

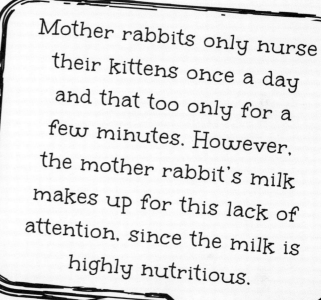

15

WHO ARE YOU SCARED OF?

I am scared of wolves, foxes, eagles, bobcats, weasels, hawks, owls and other meat-eating animals. Humans also scare me, since they hunt me for my fur and meat.

HOW DO YOU ESCAPE YOUR PREDATORS?

When chased by a predator, we hide or **scamper** away quickly. We also make quick and irregular movements to confuse our enemy.

A new word to learn

scamper - run in quick light steps

HOW BIG IS YOUR FAMILY?

We have a huge family; there are over 40 known and recognised species of rabbits in the Leporidae family.

Bunnies purr when they are happy, especially when they are being petted or stroked. Their purring sounds like the chattering of teeth.

White Albino Hare

How are Rabbits Different from Hares?

We are different from hares with regard to our life history, size and our preferred habitat. We are also smaller in size and have shorter ears than hares.

Holland Lop Rabbit

DO PET RABBITS GET BORED?

Yes! Just like humans, rabbits too get bored if they are not allowed to play or do not have enough space to run around. They can become sad and lonely.

Providing lots of toys to pet rabbits keeps them happy and helps them remain active and healthy.

ARE YOU FACING EXTINCTION?

A new word to learn

Extinction - dying out completely

Almost half of the rabbit species in the world are facing the threat of extinction. Several of us can be categorised as one of the most vulnerable mammals.

ACTIVITY TIME

BUNNY DOORKNOB

Things You'll Need

- 2 pieces of ribbons
(0.5 to 1 inch wide
and 1.5 feet long)

- Glue bottle

- Scissors

- Colourful chart paper

Draw the different parts of the Bunny doorknob on the chart paper.

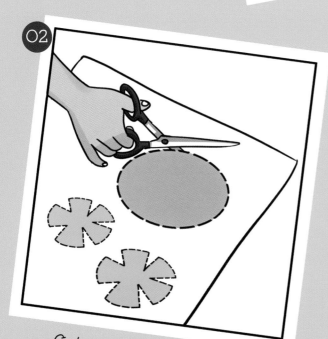

Cut out the template pieces.

Glue the Easter Bunny together. Let the Bunny dry.

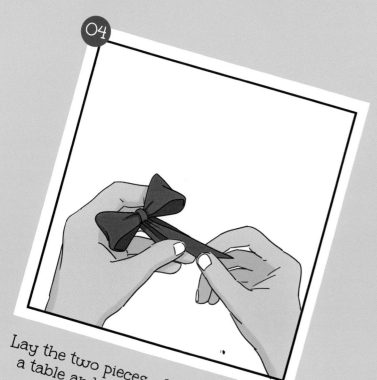

Lay the two pieces of ribbons out on a table and tie a bow on the top to attach the pieces together.

Now, glue the bow on to the Bunny's belt

Stencil sketch HOP three times on a coloured chart paper.

Cut out the HOP pieces and glue them to the Bunny.

The Bunny doorknob is ready!

The bunny is hungry.
Help it reach the carrot!